Simply People

Getting the best out of life

By

Susan Clayton

Photographics by Vicki Clayton

Published by
the space between
Upper Steanbridge Mill, Slad, Stroud
Gloucestershire, GL6 7QE
England
Telephone: 01981 580040   Fax: 01981 580030
Email: office@thespacebetween.com
Website: www.thespacebetween.com

ORDERING INFORMATION

Individual sales: All publications can be ordered direct from the space between publishing, contact details above, and through book retailers.

Quantity sales: Special discounts are available on quantity purchases by corporations, associations and others. For details contact 'Special Sales' at the space between publishing address above.

Trade purchases: Trade prices are available for book shop sales. For details contact 'Trade Purchases' at the space between publishing address above.

Printed in the UK on acid-free paper

A catalogue record for this book is available from the British Library.
ISBN 0-9538559-3-7

Cover design, photographics and typesetting by Waimanu Creative Design
Printed and bound in Great Britain by Bath Press, Bath.

The cover design is a photograph of the feet of Vicki's two year old son, Joshua.

An Invitation

Simply People is the first in a series of three books written to provide simple and accessible information about how we can be more aware and able in the way that we relate and interact with others.

Following in the series are *Simply Feedback* (what it means to be living in a world of feedback) and *The Art of People* (discovering the more complex nature of people in a simple way). All three books will be written in a similar style with accessibility, imagination and imagery.

For more information about the Simply People series and other publications by *the space between* we invite you to visit our web site.

www.thespacebetween.com

Introduction

Many books have been written on people skills, relationship skills and communication. This book is different. It provides a simple and basic understanding of the main principles that underpin all forms of human communication in any culture.

I believe that living is about people and relationships. Where quality of life is deeply affected by the quality of interactions with the world and with the people that we meet, from our close intimate relationships through to brief, one-off encounters. Our lives unfold and intertwine as we live each moment, each day.

I am curious about life and the unfolding drama. In my explorations and experimenting I have dug deep to discover what is at the root of inter-personal communication. I have learned how to live beautifully through many wise teachers. I have come to appreciate difference and to acknowledge human frailty. I am still learning.

What I have discovered I share with you in this book.

Sue Clayton

This book asks to be read
and to be lived.

Section I
DISCOVERING
WHO WE ARE

The way that we relate to people has two specific elements, **what** we do and **how** we do it - the content and the process of all our interactions.

Content is the unfolding storyline of our lives.

Process of interaction is the creation and the co-creation of all our relationships. This process also defines who we are.

Process is much less visible or audible to us than content. We have to search for it in different ways.

WHO ARE YOU?

One way of discovering who we are is to look inside ourselves and 'self reflect'. This is the root of awareness.

We also need to balance this by looking at ourselves in relation to others, by treating our world as one great big mirror in which we can see many reflections of ourselves. Without others we are unable to see these reflections. We experience this reflective behaviour in many ways, much of the time out of our awareness. For example;

- if we enjoy debate people will engage with us in debate and discussion
- if we are lively and full of fun, then the chances are that we will evoke fun and liveliness in others; they will enjoy our company
- if we care about ourselves other people will care about us too. The opposite also happens; if we don't care about ourselves then we might find that others don't give us the level of caring that we would like to have
- if we are feeling stressed, some people around us will probably show signs of stress also
- if we deny certain feelings and emotions in ourselves the chances are that when we see these emotions in others we will feel uncomfortable.

A client of mine shared with me that he felt uncomfortable talking about himself in front of other people, although he claimed that he felt alright in one-to-one conversation. When asked, he also realised that when other people talk openly about themselves in a group, especially their innermost selves, that he feels a strong sense of dislike towards them.

My client had a number of relationship difficulties that he had not understood. His awareness of himself helped him to understand how he was contributing to his own struggles.

This mirroring process moulds and shapes our relationships. It also reinforces who we are.

Our response to others and their response to us is what makes us the people that we are today; we are the sum of all our relationship.

POLAR OPPOSITES

An interesting phenomenon that occurs in relationships is where extreme behaviours exist which are mirrored as polar opposites. For instance if you are fairly chaotic in the way that you live your life you might find yourself with a partner who consistently acts in a highly organised manner.

These extremes can have a balancing effect on a relationship as well as providing the relationship with a much wider range of skills and understanding than each individual has on their own. This means that relationships at their best gain an essence that is much more than the sum of the individuals. It also means that we can learn from each other.

A few more examples of polar opposite behaviours are:

- outgoing and inward looking
- intellectual and artistic
- easy going and anxious
- talkative and quiet
- grandiose and humble
- differentiated and conforming
- pedantic and laid back

In truth many polar opposite behaviours can be an irritant in our relationships, when we fail to see their value our relationships will not 'add up' to their best.

THE OUTER AND INNER SELF

A high proportion of ourselves is relatively invisible to others; our personality, our thoughts, our history, our life experiences, our values and beliefs, our knowledge, our vulnerability, our imaginings, and so on. These become visible when we speak and when we act.

Because it is not possible for people to communicate every aspect of their inner selves all the time we have developed a human capacity to interpret, to make assumptions and to analyse situations. We need to make sense of people's behaviour in order to interact and so we begin the process.

This process can lead to misinterpretation and mis-assumption. If both people then assume that their interpretations are right, if they continue interacting without adapting and adjusting their view of each other, without revealing their inner thoughts and feelings, the quality of contact will diminish and the relationship will become difficult.

If both people in this struggle continue to avoid communicating their inner selves, what can then happen is an expectation that 'the other' will need to change for the relationship to improve.

In truth we cannot change other people we can only change ourselves;

- we can act differently so that other people respond differently towards us
- we can let other people know more about our invisible selves
- we can give other people feedback about how we are interpreting them so that they can correct us if we are wrong
- we can invite other people to tell us more about themselves
- we can become more authentic in ourselves; the more authentic we are the more we will show others our true self

Sometimes we avoid looking inside ourselves because we are afraid that what we will see we won't like.

KNOWING YOURSELF

Self awareness brings insight; that is discovering something that we didn't know before. When we have new awareness we cannot 'not know', just like we cannot unlearn how to ride a bike - although we can pretend that we don't know. In a sense this is like being told a secret; once we know the secret we can't not know it and we are probably affected by our knowing.

Like riding a bike, self awareness goes into our bones, often bringing with it fundamental change.

Knowing ourselves is:

- being able to communicate our inner experiences in our behaviour

- knowing what makes us unique – how we are similar and different to others

- understanding what drives us forward, our thirst for life, what fulfils us, our sense of purpose

- realising and throwing out old habits and beliefs that no longer serve us and replacing them with new ways of being that serve us well

- understanding how we block our own potential and then beginning to release it

- knowing our personal values and how they change with the winds of time

- realising that every time we think that we've 'cracked it' there is another discovery about ourselves yet to be uncovered

- knowing when we are stuck and when our life is flowing

- acting through CHOICE rather than being driven by habit.

Increasing self awareness is a lifetime journey.

SELF CARE

Self care is a vital part of healthy relationships. If we do not act caringly towards ourselves and nurture our own well-being, then our relationships will be affected.

> *I have had clients come to me with stress and depression, people who put all of themselves into their work and lives, asking for nothing back. They gain much respect for this, usually working in a caring profession. The one vital common factor is the lack of self care – the inability to love and care about themselves, to put themselves first – not at the expense of others (selfishly), but in balance with others.*

That means recognising that we too need support at times, to know what that is, to know how to get it, and taking special time regularly.

It is through our own self care that we are then able to give that extra bit to others.

SELF CONFIDENCE

Confidence comes with believing in ourselves and valuing who we are as a person.

We can unwittingly undermine other peoples confidence by directly relating what people DO with WHO they are as a person when they have done something wrong.

For example:

> *Two year old Zoe has been writing on the wall, her mother comes in and says that she is a bad girl, Zoe's confidence is affected because she relates badness to who she is rather than what she has been doing – and this becomes the pattern of her life if mother and authority figures continue to give her feedback in this way..*

> *If her mother had said "we do not write on walls, that is not allowed, we write on paper, let's go and find some', then Zoe learns that writing on walls is bad, not Zoe. In fact she probably feels good about herself because Mum is prepared to give her the time and find something that she can write on even though she did something that was wrong. The message is still 'I'm OK even when I do something wrong'.*

When we have been brought up feeling repeatedly bad about ourselves our self confidence becomes diminished. In adult life if we take challenging feedback as criticism we reinforce the process that was set up as a child.

Developing self-confidence means differentiating between objective feedback (what I DO) and subjective feedback (who and how I AM), relishing the delights of 'selfness'.

NOT KNOWING OURSELVES

When I reflect back on my past I realise that 'not knowing' myself created many difficulties, especially to close relationships.

When I look around me I realise that I am not alone in this, most people have been caught in the web of 'not knowing' at some time in their lives.

Some typical behaviours that I see of 'not knowing' are:

- lack of authenticity
- blaming others for personal difficulties
- criticising and judging others
- expecting others to know us
- acting out of the constraints of habit, rather than the freedom of choice
- feeling and staying stuck .

These behaviours and attitudes diminish the quality and the life of our interactions.

Knowing ourselves is a reflective process of continuous learning and discovery. What we don't know about ourselves remains a mystery until insight brings it into our self-awareness.

VULNERABILITY

When we look around we can begin to see the delicate balance in which we live, the extent of human frailty, our own personal vulnerabilities.

Our vulnerabilities are aspects of ourselves that we perceive as weakness; physically, intellectually and psychologically. Like Achilles, our perceptions make us vulnerable to becoming hurt under certain circumstances. Fortunately for most of us our Achilles heel is not fatal.

Accepting our vulnerabilities is about accepting our humanness.

Accepting our vulnerabilities can help us take care of ourselves in situations that might otherwise be damaging. Knowing our vulnerabilities enables us to protect ourselves more – or to overcome our perceptions of these weaknesses.

Paradoxically denying our vulnerabilities often highlights them, through behaviours designed to hide them away or overcome them.

The following behaviours all demonstrate areas of psychological vulnerability:

- striving for perfection
- pretending that we know something that we don't
- being judgemental and abusive towards others
- taking other people's problems on board as our own
- avoidance of conflict
- blaming others for our own mistakes
- not showing specific emotions
- making decisions based on high emotional charge
- always being in a rush, never having enough time.

Paradoxically, the more that we acknowledge and share our personal vulnerabilities, the stronger we become.

HUMILITY

When we act with humility, when we are modest and without pride, we are able to acknowledge our personal doubts and feelings. We are unpretentious; that is we do not attempt to pretend we are anything other than ourselves.

Some of the most respected people that I know act with humility. Because of this they hold a powerful and extra-ordinary presence.

Facing our humility means accepting, even delighting, in our ordinariness. Accepting how we really are will enable greater choice in how we interact with others.

In contrast, humiliation is an expression of being disregarded or shamed by others. Others may do this as a way of raising their own stakes, or of course we might do it to them. Humiliation immediately locks us into a winner/loser relationship.

When we act with humility it is not possible to be humiliated by others.

RESPONSIBILITY
OR RESPONSE-ABILITY

We each have a responsibility to ourselves and to our relationships. When we develop an *ability* to *respond* effectively and appropriately to people, to situations and to life we can manage this responsibility well.

One way of assessing our abilities to respond is to ask ourselves questions. For example how do we respond to:

- situations that don't go as planned?
- other people acting inconsiderately towards us and others?
- crisis situations?
- conflict?
- verbal attack?
- emotionally charged situations?
- manipulation by others?
- praise?
- making decisions that impact on others?
- taking risks?
- being cared about?
- challenging feedback?
- critical feedback?

Until we know the areas where we do not respond well,
we will not change or attempt to change.

DIMINISHED RESPONSE – ABILITY

Do you...

- blame others for things that don't go the way that you would like them to?
- act as though others are responsible for your life?
- over use the words 'can't' 'but'?
- play the victim – 'what others have done to me', 'what life has done to me'?
- act the persecutor – 'how bad or awful other people are'?
- always act the 'nice person'?
- criticise others for things that go wrong?
- manipulate others in order to get your needs met?
- say 'yes' when you really mean 'no'?
- act in ways that you believe you 'should' act rather than 'could' act?

Another way to find out how to improve our ability to respond to life's events is to ask our friends and colleagues where they believe our blind spots are.

FEEDBACK

We are always in a state of feedback right down to the smallest action, every single moment of our waking lives;

- we are informed by others words and actions and others are informed by our words and actions

- we take action in relation to other people's actions

- we respond to the conditions of the world about us.

This happens on an individual level a collective level, with groups, and communities. Our feedback loops are constantly changing, complex patterns of interactions.

Given the situation that we are all in it makes sense that we focus effort into developing skilful abilities to;

- convey accurate and useful information on which others can effectively act

- invite quality feedback from others in order to learn ourselves

- be fully aware of how we accept and block feedback from others.

Feedback is such an important life force that I have written another book in this series called SIMPLY FEEDBACK.

We all swim in an ocean of feedback, there is no escape.

Section 2
CREATING AND CO-CREATING RELATIONSHIPS

I invite you to consider that the making of
a relationship is a creative process and a
co-created reality

AND that we can make a difference.

'We do not grasp that we are invisible. We do
not realise that we are in a world of invisible
people. We do not understand that life, before
all other definitions of it, is a drama of the
visible and the invisible.'

Maurice Nicoll (1952)
Psychological Commentaries

HERE AND NOW

I remember being quite confused when I was first introduced to the concept of 'here and now'. I thought that it was some 'flower power' idea from the 60's that got left behind. What I discovered was a fertile and powerful component of engaging with people fully and authentically. I came to realise that *this moment* is the closest I can ever get to reality and that 'here and now' awareness feeds into healthy relating, whoever I am interacting with.

'Here and now' simply means *in this time and place*. So at this moment, as we are reading this book, IS the here and now for you.

Of course our 'here and now' also carries with it;

- our memories of past experiences

- our future expectations

- our imaginings of things taking place at the same time as now but elsewhere.

The idea of being in the here and now does not assume that we can live in the present moment without these. They all play an important role. For instance if we have a goal that we want to achieve, doing things to achieve our goal happens now. Equally the past informs us, enabling us to become more sophisticated and qualitative in our interactions in the present moment.

In truth we cannot escape from here and now
— we only imagine that we can.

NOT HERE AND NOT NOW

Strange as it may seem when we interact with others a great deal of our attention is given to 'the not here and now' – to out there and then. Notice your interactions with others and see how often this happens.

The 'NOT here' and 'NOT now' is talking or thinking about a different **place** and **time**. For example, right now we might say 'I wonder what so-and-so is doing now?'. That is *the same time* but thinking of someone in a different **place**.

A different **time** from now can only be past or future. We will either be talking about or reflecting on something that happened in the past or imagining something that may happen in the future. It is what we do now that makes us unique rather than what we are going to do tomorrow.

Our ability to attend to life that isn't in the here and now is critical to our existence. It enables us to imagine the future in order to act towards achieving our hearts desires. It enables us to learn from our past experiences. We could not live as human beings today if we did not have this ability. However we do not always serve ourselves well. When our greatest power and richness is in the moment many of us continue to live much of our lives thinking of good times or regretting the past, imagining a better future and wishing we were somewhere else – leaving us feeling disempowered.

In our quest for quality relationships we must treat the 'here and now' as our closest and most valued companion.

BELIEFS AND VALUES

When I ask people about their beliefs and values I often get blank looks as though I am talking gobbledygook - or religion. But when I ask 'what's important to you in the way that you live your life and in the way others live their lives' people respond with enthusiasm.

Often passed down from generation to generation, many of our beliefs and values are in our bones years before we are able to articulate them. Identifying our values helps us to live by them and to know what choices are available to us when faced with a conflict of values.

One way that we can identify our hidden values and beliefs is by asking 'why' questions in relation to your activities. For example right now I could ask myself 'why am I writing this book about people and relationships in this simplified way?'. My response leads to a series of further questions;

> "I want to share what I have learned about relationships in a way that is easily accessible".
>
> Why?
>
> "I believe that aspiring towards quality in relationships is important *(first belief statement)* I also believe that when we put our hearts truly into discovering and learning about relationships we begin to heal the wounds that scar our social and physical world". *(Second belief statement and also indicating a value of learning and of humanity).*
>
> So why am I writing this book in this particular style?
>
> "I like the novelty in different". *(Valuing difference)*

In doing this exercise for yourself I would encourage you to reflect on specific actions and behaviours, rather than generalisations. So instead of asking 'Why do I go to work?' ask yourself 'why am I doing this particular work in this particular place?' Keep asking why questions until you cannot go any farther.

Although we tend not to talk about our beliefs and values in everyday conversation they are powerful motivators in directing and shaping our lives and relationships.

Living in a

world of matter

Living in a sacred land

RESPECTING DIFFERENT BELIEFS AND VALUES

In relationships people tend to find that their social circles connect through shared beliefs and values. Yet holding different beliefs and values does not have to impede relationships, in fact it can add great qualities.

Respecting difference and seeking to share and discover difference can offer a rich and rewarding path of discovery.

Respecting different beliefs and values does not mean changing our own belief system, it simply means that we acknowledge a different viewpoint on life.

Respecting different values and beliefs is like looking at the same mountain from different perspectives.

AWARENESS

Awareness is at the hub of good relationships.

Awareness is our ability to engage with the infinite amount of information available both inside and outside of us.

The magic of awareness is that we can call up new data at any time, it is unlimited.

We ARE limited by the amount that we are able to hold in awareness at any give moment – AND by our fears and imagination.

Other people's awareness is completely invisible to us, that is unless they tell us. But we will never know everything that goes on inside another person, however intimate our relationship is. We can only imagine.

Awareness is not fixed in time, it travels with us, moment, by moment. It only ever exists in the 'here and now'.

BLOCKING AWARENESS

Sometimes we block our awareness of ourselves and our experiences, either through low self esteem or tough past experiences, because they are too emotionally traumatic and difficult for us to cope with – yet the data is always there to be discovered and challenged.

Increasing awareness leads to greater choice in how we interact with others and the world around you.

LEVELS OF AWARENESS

We all have many levels of awareness and it seems to me that as we get older our awareness expands and deepens. At a simple level, different aspects of awareness include inner awareness, outer awareness and an awareness of our self in context.

Inner awareness is

- in our senses, seeing, hearing, tasting, smelling, touching.
- in bodily sensations and movement
- in our thoughts
- in emotions and feelings
- in insight
- in intuition and knowing

Outer awareness is the context and rich environment in which our own personal life drama unfolds. It includes;

- awareness of minute detail in our natural environment, for example the pattern in a slow flake, through to the expansiveness of the infinite universe
- awareness of social rules and norms (enabling us all to co-exist)
- awareness of our family setting (creating society through family structures)
- awareness of continuous change, for instance the changing environment, social change and technological change
- awareness of people and patterns of behaviour that we come into contact with in our daily life.

Self in context is the meeting of our inner and outer world, the reaction and response between us and our environment; between us and the people that we meet.

There are differences between us in our desire to increase our awareness, there is no right or wrong – awareness just IS.

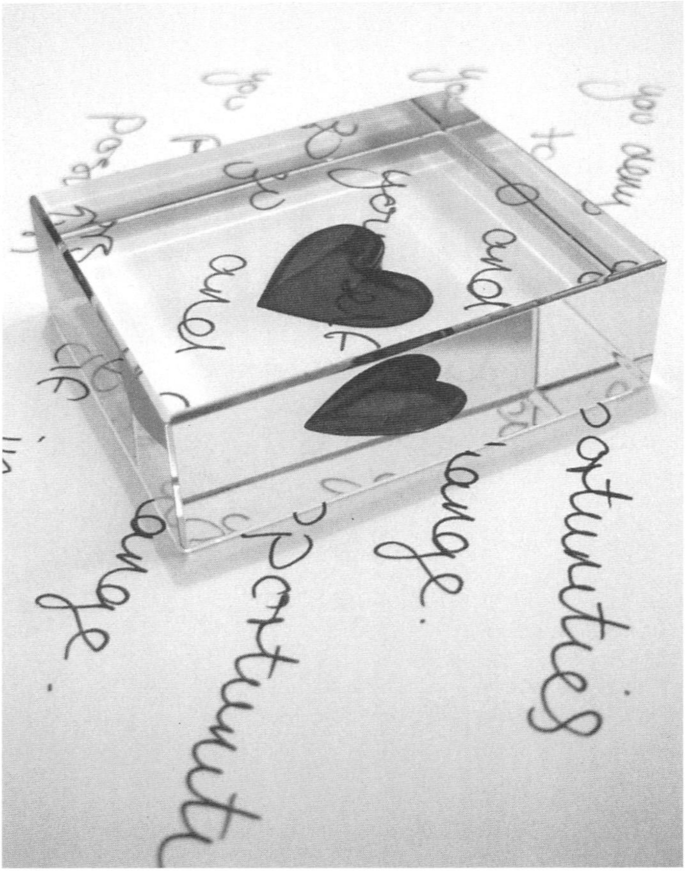

CARING FOR

There are two different aspects of caring: Caring FOR and Caring ABOUT. There is a fundamental difference between them, yet many people get them confused.

When we care FOR someone we DO things for them that they otherwise cannot do for themselves, you could say that we take on a caring role. When we misplace caring ABOUT someone with caring FOR someone we are doing our relationship a dis-service;

- we create a dependency on us from the other person

- we put ourselves in a superior position over the other person (we do this by acting as though they are unable to do the things that we do for them)

- we deny the other person opportunities to grow and change

- we deny ourselves opportunities to grow and change.

I know of many people (in fact many women) who put value on who they are through the extent to which they nurture others, it is almost like a parenting role that has become stuck. They spend their lives caring FOR others and consequently do not feel cared ABOUT.

Paradoxically, only caring FOR people without balancing this with self care or being cared ABOUT by others, can have an affect on the health of the carer.

we are able to find equality
in relationships,
even if others hold a higher status.
or low status to theirs

CARING ABOUT

Caring ABOUT someone is BEING caring as opposed to DOING caring.

Caring about someone doesn't always mean being nice; sometimes caring means being tough with people.

Our ability to show that we care can be expressed in many ways:

- we are willing to challenge and confront the people who we care about on personal and professional issues

- we are able to face possible conflict with them

- we are able to discuss with them issues that block the quality of the contact that we have with each other

- we are able to find equality in our relationship, even if our role is higher status, or lower status to theirs

- we are able to show others our vulnerabilities as well as our strengths

- we are able to tell others that we care and behave in ways that are caring

- we challenge gossip and rumour

- we choose to offer support in difficult situations rather than stand by and watch

- we bring our own humility into our relationships with others.

In quality relationships we can DO caring and BE caring at the same time. We can care ABOUT someone and at the same time care FOR them, as we do with children, and in phases of dependency with our partners, friends and relations.

EMPATHY

A critical component of establishing quality relationships is being able to develop some understanding of other people's experiences. This is 'putting ourselves in the other person's shoes'. That is, understanding and imaginatively entering into another person's world.

The more that we have had similar experiences with others, the more that we are able to empathise and walk along beside them on common ground. However we will never know exactly what another person is thinking and experiencing simply because our inner worlds are all so different – even when we know people well and can predict and anticipate them, we can never enter their entire inner world. So understanding has much to do with imagining and attempting to make sense, rather than knowing a truth.

The more that we experience life the greater the degree of empathy we are able to offer in return.

SYMPATHY

I have noticed that sometimes people are confused between sympathy and empathy.

Sympathy is when *we share* in another's emotions in the moment, particularly emotions such as pity, compassion, sorrow, despair, anger, even though we may not have had a similar experience ourselves or be involved in the current situation.

This is in contrast to empathy, where we *understand* another's emotions and their situation. This understanding arises through our own similar experience in the past. In contrast to sympathy, these experiences are not confined to sad or difficult situations. If we have not had a similar experience in the past then it is difficult to fully empathise – in which case it is helpful to say so rather than to pretend otherwise.

Misplacing sympathy for empathy, that is assuming that we fully understand because we feel the emotion, lacks authenticity.

I'm a strawberry

AUTHENTICITY

For a long time I wasn't clear what authenticity really meant. I had a hunch that it meant being honest with ourselves and others. I now realise that it is more than that.

Being authentic is matching our outer selves, *what we say and how we say* it and *what we do and how we do it*, with our invisible selves, *our values, beliefs, viewpoint and inner feelings*, in our contact with others.

So when we are fully authentic we are being true to ourselves and to others. There is consistency in our message. This is a challenging quest, it means that we will need to become more aware of ourselves. It means developing an ability to self-reflect, to understand ourselves, our needs, our feelings, how we do things and why we do them.

Authenticity reduces the possibility of mis-interpretation and mis-understanding in relationships and increases trust.

Your authenticity will encourage others to be authentic with you.

Having awareness about our feelings and being able to express them is the key to being authentic.

I'm a strawberry

INAUTHENTIC

When we are being inauthentic we are acting in a way that isn't a true expression of our inner thoughts, values and feelings. This happens for three reasons:

- we might not be fully in touch with what is going on inside us
- we might be afraid of being fully open with the other person.
- we might not know how to be fully open with the other person.

Yet there are many ways to communicate a true expression of our inner thoughts and experiences because there is so much going on. Being selective allows us to reveal what is appropriate and most present. It isn't a matter of 'either, or'. For instance if I am feeling frustrated the choices I have are:

- saying that I am feeling frustrated and what is causing that for me
- to show my frustration and say how I would like things to change
- to relate my frustrations with the here and now "I don't normally get frustrated over this but right now that's how I feel".

We can usually tell when people are being inauthentic their behaviour does not match with what they say. Even if we don't notice inconsistencies we will probably feel a discomfort, although we may not immediately attribute this to lack of authenticity of the other person.

Some people are very skilled at hiding their inner selves from the outside world, especially if;

- they fear being rejected, humiliated or not appreciated by the other person;
- they do not value themselves and therefore believe that others won't value them either.

When others appear to be inauthentic, we can encourage them to become more authentic with us by being authentic yourself.

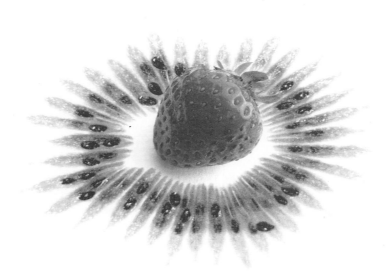

BUILDING AUTHENTIC RELATIONSHIPS

Authenticity in relationships leads to greater transparency. We are able to see each other more, understand each other and make fewer mistakes in reading each other.

As well as being authentic ourselves we can help to build our relationships when we see that others are not being truly authentic with us.

One way of doing this is to say what we observe, picking up on the inconsistency and commenting on what we imagine is happening for the other person;

> 'You say that you are happy about the decision but you don't sound happy. I imagine that you are really quite disappointed'.

Responding in this way is relatively easy. Thinking about responding like this, or taking the risk to do it is often where we need to put extra thought and attention.

Authentic relationships are co-created.

INTEGRITY

When we have integrity we are carrying and expressing moral and social values. That is, values that support the good of individuals, communities and society. We act in a way that supports both ourselves and others and we pay attention to the impact of our actions on others.

We all have the capacity to act with integrity. Most of us do a great deal of the time.

However life isn't always that straightforward. There are times when we act in a way that we feel is with integrity and we later discover that things didn't work out as intended:

- Different people have different needs, some of which conflict. For example trying to 'please everyone' at Christmas or times of family celebration rarely works.

- We provide support for someone only to discover some time later that they hadn't really appreciated it. In which case perhaps we made assumptions about their needs and acted on them, without checking them out.

Integrity means that our intent is moral and acted on. With moral intent comes a willingness to appreciate when we get it wrong and how we can increasingly become more open about our actions so that others are able to interact and inform our future decisions.

When integrity is outstanding we see people acting totally unconditionally; there is no expectation or requirement for something in return.

LACK OF INTEGRITY

When we act in a way that lacks integrity we will do things at the expense of others or without consideration of the impact that our actions will have on others or on the environment.

We lack integrity when we are driven to act purely on personal desires;

- for money, status, possessions, sex, power

- to win, to get recognition, to be loved

- to avoid being seen for who we really are, or avoid being caught out for our misdoings

- through fear of losing something that is important to us.

People who lack integrity are often masters at manipulating others in order to get their own needs met. But they also need people who are naive, gullible or who will not challenge them to achieve this, that then becomes the co-created relationship.

VALUING DIFFERENCE

We are all different. Difference is visible through our skin colour, hair, facial features, physical build and dress. The invisible difference is in our beliefs, values, history, knowledge, abilities, memories, mind sets, imagination, established patterns of behaviour and processes for understanding our world.

It is also true, given that we have evolved as social creatures, that we naturally seek belonging rather than isolation and we frequently do that by looking for similarities and common ground.

Yet, in established relationships it is the tapestry of difference; experiences, skills, abilities, knowledge, views of the world, and personal character, that breathes life into those relationships.

Avoidance of difference in a relationship, and a continued push towards sameness is driven by fear, as is a desire to always be different.

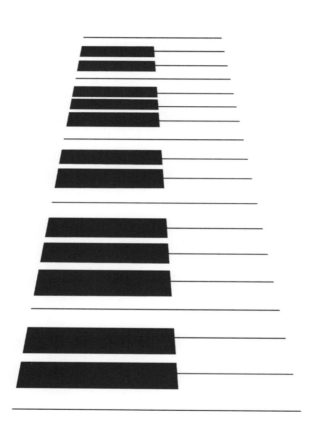

DIFFICULT RELATIONSHIPS

Our lack of understanding of difference, and mis-assumptions about each other can lead to all sorts of difficulties. The entanglements and conflict that arise from these difficulties can be daunting. Some particularly difficult relationships matter to us, some we might feel are not worth putting the effort into resolving.

Resolving difficult relationships takes energy, thought and self reflection. I try to take the view that IT ISN'T THE PERSON THAT IS DIFFICULT IT IS THE RELATIONSHIP THAT'S DIFFICULT, which means that I am also contributing to this difficulty and that I need to understand what I do that adds to the difficulty.

In these situations I usually discover that I have not fully understood the other person and neither have I felt understood by them. This can happen for a number of reasons:

- our differences do not allow us to have any degree of empathy with each other's position.

- we are seeking commonality on opposing issues rather than valuing difference on our diverse viewpoints.

- our differences (beliefs, values, viewpoints) are not being mutually respected.

Resolving difficulties usually isn't about seeking similarity or acknowledging difference, it is about finding a dynamic balance between the two.

All relationships have some degree of difficulty. The difficulty in relationships provide us with an opportunity to develop and refine our own behaviour, to see our imperfections, and to fine tune our relationship skills.

IMAGINATION

Imagination is a powerful gift when we know it, care for it, feed it and release it.

- Many people connect imagination to the arts, I also connect it to the moment by moment experience because that is where it is truly at its best in building quality relationships.

- Imagination can be fun, novel, interesting, evocative, momentary, amusing, insightful, wise.

- Children need imagination to grow and develop. Imaginary friends are a wonderful example. Sadly many adults keep the door of this cage shut for fear of losing control.

- In the workplace imagination is often deadened or confined to a box of 'brainstorming ideas'. Yet imagination is with us all the time. Our challenge is to see it, hear it, respond to it, engage with it, free it and delight in it.

- Relationships come alive through imaginative interaction.

- Imagination can be the source of great anxiety and fear if we are unable to distinguish it from reality. Most people have experienced anxiety and fear on the cusp between waking and a bad dream – the imagination of the unconscious.

- Ideology and grandiosity are imagination untamed.

- Imagination puts zest into our life drama as drama renews imagination in our life. It has a magical spirit.

Imagination is the space between fact and fiction.

IMAGINING RELATIONSHIPS

Through imagination we construct hopes and aspirations, which provide a map to guide us towards achieving them. When our hopes and aspirations are not achievable, for instance based on ideology or grandiosity, or filled with dogma (fixed rules and beliefs) then relationships fail.

I have at times heard people speak of their friends who 'have a perfect relationship' only to be surprised some time later that the couple have split up. When this happens 'perfection' is ideological, based on the belief that ideal relationships have no conflict, no arguments and present an external image of 'true love'. Imagining that such a relationship could survive is idealistic.

People break up and marriages break down because they were based on ideological constructs rather than achievable aspirations. Deep intimate relationships do not just happen, they take years of continuous work. Yet many people are spellbound in romantic relationships hoping that they can achieve their ideal by getting married or in living together. Then feel let down by their partner (or the whole of the opposite gender) when the ideal state is not achieved.

Paradoxically breaking the spell, which means changing ideological beliefs about marriage and romance, can achieve lasting and rewarding relationships.

Relationships need conflict and difference in order to develop
a robustness that will enable them to survive.

Section 3
THE LANGUAGE IN RELATING

Voice

$\oint_4^4$ thoughts

ωορδ ϖοιχε
τηουγητσ

LANGUAGE & READING BETWEEN THE LINES

We have a tapestry of languages in the world and the spoken word brings alive the content of life and the gift of thought. Language provides a means of conveying thought and information.

Thought of course is invisible until we share it. This is useful to us as it allows us to think through what we want to say before we say it.

In our interactions with others we need to seek a balance between over-editing our thoughts which can take the spontaneity out of life, and no editing, which can result in a long trail of gibberish which is difficult for others to absorb.

Sometimes we simply do not have the vocabulary to say what we want to say.

Sometimes we try to use the spoken word to boost our self-image.

Sometimes we simply talk too much.

Language is not just the spoken word. Language is also in;
- voice and intonation
- stance and body movement
- expression in the face and eyes
- level of interest in the interaction
- clothes
- the context and history
- the quality of the contact
- and the unspoken words – what is absent from the spoken language
- silence.

Spoken words are never isolated from the greater
language of our wholeness.

BEYOND CLICHÉS

Clichés are re-cycled and overused words and statements which generally go back a long time in history.

Clichés can be a gift in the art of relating or they can bring a relationship to its knees through boredom.

In the art of relating clichés provide a route through which we can begin to engage with people lightly, either when we meet with a person for the first time or when simply brushing shoulders.

When used imaginatively clichés can express exactly the point that we want to make.

In bored relationships clichés often function as a guard against personal or intimate contact.

Some people have an extraordinary ability to talk in clichés – they can be utterly boring.

Here are a few common clichés;

- we don't see eye to eye
- having said that
- it will all come out in the wash
- keep your chin up
- needless to say
- neither here nor there
- quality of life
- over the top
- now or never
- that's life
- this day and age

We can enhance the language of relating by using clichés choicefully and imaginatively, rather than through habit.

The language of silence

Silent Language	Example
Listening	"I am listening to you and noticing you with curiosity, interest, compassion, or intrigue, and have nothing to say yet".
Mis-trust	"I want to say something but I don't feel safe enough to say it".
Self editing	"I want to say something but I am not clear or precise enough in what I want to say"
Reflective	"I am taking time out to contact my inner self and to reflect on my thoughts".
Passive aggressive	"I am feeling angry with you and remain silent as an expression of my anger".
Thoughtful	"I am trying to make sense of this in order to know how to respond".
Emotional	"I am feeling too hurt to know what to say".
Shy	"I want to say something but don't want to be seen".
Overwhelmed	"I have something to say but find it difficult to interrupt others".
Low self esteem	Belief that 'you will not value what I have to say' – which comes form 'What I have to say is not of value'.
Meditative	Using the moment to meditate.
Bored	"I am bored with this situation, with you, with myself but unwilling to act in order to change the situation".
Soporific	"I feel low energy or sleepy".
Detached	"I am unable or unwilling to connect with the discussion".

SILENCE

Silence has many meanings, in the language of relationships our challenge is to understand the range of expressions that go with silence.

On the one hand silence is a reflective time, an observing time, a listening time. In the fast pace of the 21st century it seems that we do not allow ourselves enough silence. On the other hand silence is a message for others to make meaning of.

Sometimes when people are silent they convey the most important message in that moment – so often this message is missed and then mis-understandings occur.

Silence is only ever here and now.

Discovering the meaning of the silence is an art.

There is always language and meaning in silence. Our challenge is to hear, notice and discover what is being communicated AND what is being withheld.

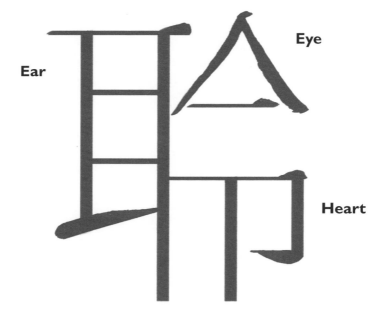

Ear

Eye

Heart

LISTENING

Good listening isn't just hearing, it is selecting the relevance and meaning from what we are hearing. That means listening to what IS NOT being said as well as to what IS being said.

Today's fast pace and busy chatter leaves little space for good listening and to be listened to. This means that we respond to what we 'hear'; words without the full meaning in the language. When we slow down and truly listen we hear more than words, we discover the expansiveness and minutiae of what is being said.

When we truly listen we dampen our own chatter so that we too give more by talking less. Our ability to listen is a gift to the people that we listen to, to ourselves and to our relationships.

When we ask to be listened to in a caring way, usually people will listen. The choice, and the risk, is in asking.

To listen IS quality.

SECRETS, GOSSIP AND THE GRAPEVINE

Life is full of secrets and gossip. They are an essential part of communication, of passing information on, of making meaning and understanding.

Our ancestors relied on the grapevine for communication. Yet the grapevine is often used as an outlet for revenge and destruction on people and relationships; where venom and poison travel through the veins of the vine at great speed. This would not be the case if, in our daily lives we allowed ourselves to confront venomous chatter and complete issues that are difficult to deal with.

Dealing with rumour and gossip can be a challenge because it often brings with it mystery and alluring drama. Once we have overcome the allure we can act responsibly by;

- questioning why we are being invited to receive this information
- questioning ourselves "Is this a secret that I am prepared to keep?"
- questioning the level of confidentiality surrounding the secret, and our ability to act with integrity
- acting choicefully and taking full responsibility for the consequences of our actions
- acting according to our personal and social values.

If our curiosity gets the better of us, or we hear a piece of gossip before we have the chance to stop it, then we need to know that we still have some choice in how we deal with it. For instance;

- we can challenge the integrity of the person who gave it to us and question the real value of the piece of gossip and the impact on the people involved.
- we can choose to ignore it.
- we can ask the messenger why they are telling us.

When someone tells us a secret or a piece of gossip we can't not know it and we have a responsibility for what we do with it.

yesterday...

FACT AND FICTION

What is fact and what is fiction? Much of our life is factional; that is, a combination of fact and fiction. So what is fact and what is fiction?

- Our inner self is fact; what we feel, experience, observe, hear, touch, taste, smell, think.
- The present moment is fact.
- Imaginings are fiction.
- What does not exist in the here and now is fiction, which can be based on fact.
- History – our very own past experience – becomes intermingled with fictional threads. We exaggerate in order to build the drama, to paint the picture. Our perception is different to other peoples yet our storylines become influenced by other people's experiences.
- Have you ever noticed that as you grow older you see your past in a different way. As memories fade we fill the gaps with the closest match, or the match that we want to fit the space. Our storyline changes according to who we are talking to – yet we are convincing even to ourselves.
- We speculate about what was and is going on for other people. But we act as though we KNOW it. When we do this we do others an injustice.
- Imagining only ever happens 'here and now'. Serious relationship problems can arise when distorted imaginings are held as true and acted upon.
- Negative thoughts carry a great deal of fiction, left unchecked they can be extremely destructive, as many people know who have experienced broken personal relationships. Such imaginings held as truths can lie dormant for generations, carrying bitter consequences, until honesty, love and compassion challenge the strongly held beliefs.

It seems that our lives contain much more fiction than fact.

KNOWLEDGE

We all have knowledge, and knowing. Until we reveal it to the world it is invisible. Knowledge and knowing come in many forms;

Wisdom Wisdom is like wine; the grapes of knowledge fermented by experience. Knowledge alone is not wisdom.

Sometimes we are scared of other people's wisdom.

Experience Life experiences are the essence of wisdom. The more experiences that we have in life, the greater our wisdom.

Intuition Intuition comes from our instincts. Because intuition is not logical it is often not supported in decision making processes in the global world today. Yet intuition provides information that is not in the logical mind. Because of this, intuition can appear magical. It is a powerful resource.

We all have intuition, the issue is do we trust it? Paradoxically the more we trust our own intuition the more we learn to trust the intuition of others.

Intuition guides us to the obvious, to the unseen, and to meeting the rejected part of our relationships.

Facts In life we are surrounded by data and information, our challenge is to differentiate between fact and fiction.

Sensing Making sense of life and relationships is using all of our senses to make meaning, not just our logic.

Beliefs There are times when we believe in something so strongly that we just KNOW.

Our greater knowledge is invisible much of the time

NOT KNOWING

Because knowledge is invisible it is possible to pretend that we know something when in reality we don't. We all do it or have done it some time in our lives, sometimes to hide our ignorance or naivety, sometimes through fear of humiliation or loss of respect.

Some people never reveal their 'not knowing'. Their lack of authenticity gives them away.

Paradoxically, wisdom embraces the world of not knowing.
That is, our ability to reveal 'that we don't know' is wiser
than pretending that we do.

UNDERSTANDING

Language of any kind requires understanding in order for it to work, and so does the language of relationships.

The way that we acquire understanding is through bringing together fact and fiction, by drawing on all that we understand, and then interpreting what we don't yet understand in order to make sense.

We have a natural desire to seek completion, to fill the gaps when they are missing in order to establish meaning and to see the whole picture. Perhaps you can imagine how that process can lead to mis-reading or mis-hearing language, especially when the information that is coming through is lacking key data. Take a look at the drawings on the left and notice how the eye seeks to complete the images.

What this tells us is that in seeking understanding we make sense through patterns and filling in the gaps. That is the same with any form of language throughout the world including the language of music and art.

In relationships, problems can arise when we attempt to engage with very little information available, when communication is constrained. This will happen when there is little trust between two people. Yet trust builds through understanding.

The advent of E-mail has highlighted the 'missing pieces' problem. In my view it is even more tricky to understand and resolve relationship difficulties through E-mail because they are so open to misinterpretation.

In today's fast moving world people expect fast moving information and immediate clarity. This process interrupts the richness of waiting when situations are cloudy. We feel pulled towards forcing understanding.

ASSUMPTIONS

Assumptions help us to engage with the world and with people. It is the starting point – not the finish point. Pitfalls arise when we believe we are at the finish point, when we act as though our assumptions are correct when in fact they need checking, adapting and adjusting.

We need to take some things for granted, but when we recognise this and accept the risk involved in taking people for granted we can be more conscious of our assumptions and begin to check them out.

Checking assumptions means;

- asking important clarification questions like "what do you mean by that?"
- if you don't understand, to say so
- asking ourselves if the information we have been given is useful and reliable
- checking if limits are being imposed unnecessarily
- checking out inconsistencies
- noticing any expectations that are being imposed.
- noticing when we assume that others have the same view as we do
- checking facts when they have been given second hand.

The process of checking assumptions adds to the quality of relationships simply because people feel heard. If we balance this by providing good detail about ourselves to enable more accurate assumptions by others, that too can increase trust, as well as improve communication.

Assumptions help us to engage with the world and with people. It is the starting point – not the finish point.

it won't work

you never listen

he will never

you don't understand listen

we always do that

he will never agree

there's no other way

you must be...

it can't be

we will never agree

it can't agree

we wouldn't be changed

you must be...

there's no

other way

MIS-ASSUMPTIONS

There is nothing wrong with making mis-assumptions, it is part of our discovery process. Any assumption, however accurate or not, enables us to calibrate our understanding of a situation and of other people.

If we mistakenly assume that we understand people and act on these mis-assumptions we will likely encounter unexpected difficulties, waste time and effort, feel confused, face potential conflict and feel mis-understood.

When we make this mistake we will say things like;

- 'he will never agree'
- 'we always do that'
- 'you don't understand'
- 'you never listen'
- 'there's no other way'
- 'you must be...'
- 'it can't be changed'
- 'we wouldn't be allowed'
- 'it won't work'

It can be productive to check assumptions when we are experiencing relationship difficulties, the chances are that incorrect assumptions are being made by both people.

Section 4
THE DRAMA IN RELATING

The drama in relationships is created
through the emotions that drive the
interplay between people.

Miserable Frustrated Disappointed

Imaginative Aimless Cold Cautious Generous

Hot Envious Creative Disgusted Happy Sad

Innocent Awful

Confident Surprised Fearful Bewildered Pained Fuzzy

Humiliated Trusting Lost Suspicious

Horrified Cold Aimless Upset Angry Idiotic

FEELINGS

We have many feelings. I do not believe that people cannot show their feelings. I do believe that all of us struggle to understand and show some feelings. Some people have more on their list than others.

Anxious	Frustrated	Optimistic
Apologetic	Fuzzy	Pained
Arrogant	Generous	Paranoid
Ashamed	Grieving	Passionate
Awe	Guilty	Perplexed
Awful	Happy	Puzzled
Bashful	Helpful	Regretful
Bewildered	Horrified	Relieved
Bored	Hot	Respectful
Cautious	Humiliated	Sad
Confident	Hurt	Satisfied
Creative	Hysterical	Shocked
Curious	Idiotic	Sheepish
Determined	Indifferent	Smug
Disappointed	Innocent	Stupid
Disgusted	Interested	Surprised
Distant	Jarred	Suspicious
Ecstatic	Jealous	Sympathetic
Embarrassed	Joyful	Tense
Energetic	Lonely	Thoughtful
Envious	Lost	Trusting
Exasperated	Loving	Undecided
Excited	Mischievous	Undervalued
Exhausted	Miserable	Upset
Fearful	Na ve	Valued
Frightened	Obstinate	Withdrawn

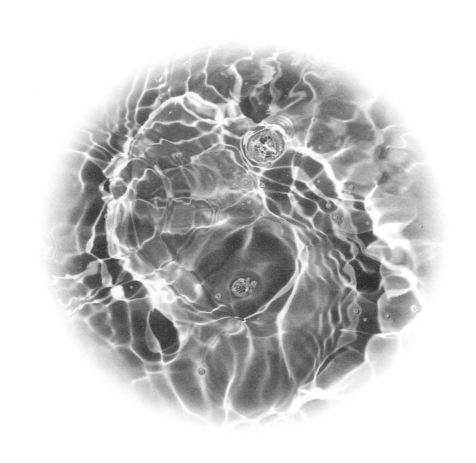

EMOTIONS (E-motion: Energy in motion)

Emotions are complex patterns of feelings. They drive our behaviour. We ALL have emotions. Our emotions arrive in our bodies - not our heads. Our ability to understand our emotions, or even to know that we feel, varies from person to person. All of us will have certain emotions that we are familiar with and some emotions that we are less familiar with.

We experience our emotions before we make sense of them so we know that they are affecting us. We probably show signs of emotions outwardly through our body. In the process of making sense of our emotions we turn them into language. Language enables us to understand ourselves and communicate this understanding verbally to others.

If we de-value our own emotions and de-value other people's emotions then our co-created reality becomes diminished and de-valued also.

Our emotions only exist in our moment by moment experience. We might remember how we felt in the past, we will anticipate how we might feel in the future but we only ever experience emotions and feelings in the present moment.

Emotions are the essence of our existence. So we need to make friends with them, to care about them and to bring all of our emotions into our life. We will then know;

- when we cannot think straight because we are emotionally full
- when our overt feelings block deeper feelings that need to be released, for example when sadness hides anger or anger hides grief.
- when to reveal our personal struggles and when to hold back.

In making friends with our emotions we also need to be a friend to our emotions. To respect their fullness, and to know those that are absent from our repertoire.

Emotions are the energy that create drama, add colour to laughter, bring excitement to a mystery, add soul into dance and invoke life into relationships.

BEHAVING IRRATIONALLY

I often wondered what my parents meant when they made reference to other people making 'irrational decisions' or acting 'irrationally'. It took me many years to realise that I also can be irrational at times — and of course so can they.

Irrational behaviour has a very strong emotional charge. On the basis that emotions drive behaviour, here is a good example of exactly that. People act on their emotional drive rather than through good reasoning, intuition or common sense. What seems to happen is that excessive emotion drowns out reasonable action.

So when we act irrationally we will be acting in a way that to others would seem illogical or even absurd. To us it might seem reasonable. So any feedback is not likely to be heard.

Can you remember times when you have fallen 'madly in love', or when you were infatuated by someone? Or, can you remember a time when you were furious with someone who acted against your wishes? When you look back did you act irrationally then or did you handle the situation with sound common sense?

If we notice when we are being driven by high emotional charge,
then it is better to avoid making decisions until our emotions
have subsided and rationality, or a sense of calm returns.

ACTING OUT OF FEAR

We all know what fear feels like. The feeling of fear is unpleasant and people's natural tendency is to avoid it rather than face it.

Fear is an emotion that is all encompassing based on imaginary thoughts of something that has not yet happened or is happening somewhere else.

The feeling of trepidation or excitement that comes with fear drives and influences our behaviour. This can be helpful to us at times, it makes us aware of potential dangers ahead, yet much fear is irrational and unfounded.

When we are fearful we might;

- be pessimistic
- cover our view of the world in a dull cloud
- carry a scarcity mentality i.e. there will never be enough money for everyone
- become cynical
- move into a duality of winning and losing and classify ourselves as a loser
- live in the past, future or somewhere else
- hold ourselves back from something that we really want to do or say and then later regret
- become stuck in reactive patterns of behaviour.

Many of our fears are out of our awareness until we begin to notice repetitive patterns in our behaviour and seek to identify what drives these behaviours.

FEAR AND RELATING

It is easier to define our life fears (for instance, fear of heights or fear of spiders) than the fears that exist in fixed patterns of inter-relating with people. Our relating fears underlie every relationship that we have with others and therefore impede our contact with them:

- fear of rejection
- fear of being mis-understood
- fear of being undervalued
- fear of being mis-perceived
- fear of being belittled or intimidated
- fear of humiliation
- fear of shame
- fear of losing the relationship
- fear of losing the battle
- fear of abuse, attack or being shouted at
- fear of abandonment
- fear of being ignored
- fear of not being seen
- fear of conflict

We react to fear in a number of different ways, some people react with aggression, some with depression, some through escapism and denial. All of these responses avoid facing our fixed patterns and beliefs that have become deeply ingrained. It takes awareness of our own behaviour patterns and understanding our innermost fears to raise them to the surface and overcome them.

I know of no-one who is fearless

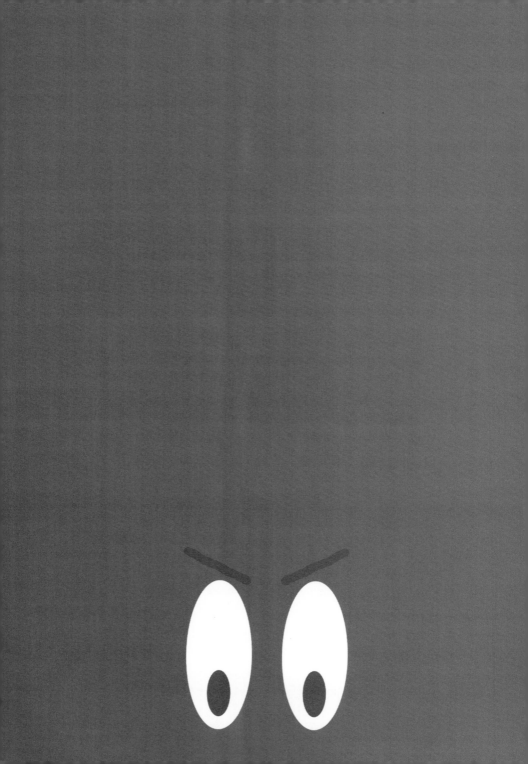

FACING FEAR

Fear is disabling to us and to our relationships because fear takes control. Turning the tide on our fears is about learning to respond to life in a different way and taking risks.

Here and now   One of the very best tools for overcoming fear in relationships is to stay in the here and now. This is such an obvious thing to do as fear is based on imaginings.

Authenticity   Bringing our authentic self into our interaction enables us to be present – being fearful is not being present. For example if we fear that we might be about to go into battle with someone we can then say to that person "I fear that I may become locked in a battle with you and I don't want that to happen". That is being authentic. By articulating our fear the relationship changes.

Reflecting   There have been times when I have walked way from a situation and regretted that I had not said or responded in a different way? Reflecting on these situations has helped me to discover in myself the fear that stopped me from responding.

We can also assist others if we notice that they are holding back. A process that I find very useful is in using the following three very simple statements:

- *What I notice (in me, in you, in this situation)*
- *What I imagine (what I think, understand, assume, speculate)*
- *What I feel (experience)*

You can turn use three statements in any order using a wide variety of language that works for you.

SHAME

Shame is a part of human existence, a means of maintaining principles standards and ethics. Yet, paradoxically it can also prevent quality relations.

Few people consider that shame might be present when relating to others. Yet I know from my own experience and in working with people that shame is like a hidden venomous creature in a beautiful garden, always there but we never know exactly when we will come across it.

The fear of feeling shame or exposing shame in others is one of the most powerful forces that inhibit contact between people, especially on sensitive, personal and intimate issues. What we don't know is what other people are sensitive to, or shameful of.

We can model a way of opening and revealing shame unashamedly;

> "I feel embarrassed to say this ..."

> "This is difficult for me to talk about and ....."

The main issue that gets in the way of bringing shame into the open and an acceptable part of everyday life is feeling ashamed of shame – so people simply do not talk about it.

Improving our relations with others means coming to terms with our own shame and also treating shame openly and lovingly.

The way forward within ourselves is to be;

- forgiving of ourselves for those things that we feel ashamed about
- forgiving of others for the times that they have inadvertently shamed us.·

Where there is no room for forgiveness for ourselves there is no opportunity for our relationships to grow.

In many cultures shame runs deep like a destructive river; love, compassion and forgiveness are the most powerful antidotes.

Feeling shame is unpleasant. We vary in our responses to shame, we therefore need to make sure that we don't make assumptions about other people's experience around shame.

LOVE

People confuse love and pleasure. There is much pleasure that people engage in that has very little love in it, and not all love is pleasurable.

- There are times that we need to be tough in order to be kind to those that we love.
- Lovingness towards others carries integrity.
- Romantic love can be wonderful – and irrational!

Unconditional love is the process of being loving and giving towards others without an expectation of something in return.

When we experience conditional love there is a voiced or implied expectation of something in return for 'love'. The relationship is imbalanced, one person is in control and using their position to manipulate the relationship to get their own personal needs met without consideration of the impact on the other person. People fall into the trap of conditional relationships out of fear.

Love is a tough challenge in life and in relationships.

LOVE AND HATE

Love and hate are often seen as the opposite polarities on the same axis. This view comes from the belief that we hate because we have loved. In many cases that is true; we feel love for a person, we simply hate what they are doing. Without love there is no hate.

We all want to be loved yet don't always see this as being the same for others. Our actions towards others can be less than loving when we are driven by selfish needs or fear. I have seen people going through separation and divorce suddenly becoming filled with hate and bitterness, when once these two people loved each other.

People often struggle to learn how to be loving when faced with conflict. What I find disturbing is that on the grapevine people tend to collude with hate rather than challenging it.

In the depths of our hearts we feel lovingness. When
we close our hearts to the world we shut our
lovingness off to others and to ourselves.

PASSION

Passion is pure energy.
It is the force that steers us towards new destinations
It is the compassion that carries us when we are faced
with hardship
It is the impulse of our journey and our destiny.
It is a lust for life.

POWER-FULL RELATIONSHIPS

Inter-relating has three different entities of power; you, the other person and the relationship. We can build a powerful relationship as much as we can weaken it.

In my own experience I notice that I feel at my most powerful when I feel able to be fully myself in the relationship. That is, where there are no constraints on the relationship by the other person or by myself. This is true for all my relationships; with my children, my partner, my family, in my work, socially.

When I do not feel powerful it is usually because an imbalance has been created either by myself or by the other person. I notice that when this happens it diminishes my power and weakens the power in the relationship. An example of this is intimidation. I know that when I feel intimidated by someone I do not feel able to be fully me and I do not feel very powerful. Although I now know that becoming timid is something that I do to myself in response to others, it still creates a power imbalance that affects both myself and the relationship if I let it happen.

The most power-full relationships are those where people value each other for who they truly are and encourage each others wholeness.

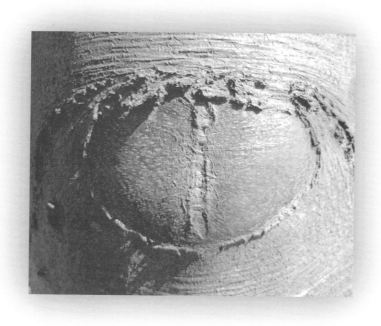

CONTROL

Control is paradoxical, the more we try to control our lives in order to get our needs met, the more we feel out of control and stressed.

The more that we let go, the more that we achieve and feel a sense of well being.

People in positions of authority, like managers, leaders, parents, teachers, who over-control as a means of achieving results or establishing clear boundaries, will get less than those who work in relationship with people with some freedom to act.

When I let go of what I am I become what I might be.

John Heider (1986)
The Tao of Leadership
Gower:England

Manipulators have many disguises that they wear [which draw you into their control]:

The hat of old friends - 'gosh you haven't changed a bit'

The blanket of a victim - 'they don't care about us'

The spectacles of a sceptic - 'don't do it, they've done all this before and it didn't work'

The sword of a persecutor - 'look what awful things they do, they've always been the same'

The shoes of an autocrat - 'do it my way and you won't go wrong'

The trousers of the master - 'you always used to do it, what's different now?'

Profiting from Diversity (1998)
Trevor Bentley & Susan Clayton

MANIPULATION

This is a form of control and involves getting ones needs met in a way that is not fully transparent. In highly political systems people learn how to manipulate in order to get results, or even survive. For some it is the only way - learn to manipulate or leave.

For many, manipulation is regarded as a negative activity because people often get caught up in it without knowing, to the advantage of the manipulator. However all we have to do is to watch children to see how skilled they are at manipulating their parents and we realise how ingrained manipulative behaviour is.

Manipulation takes many forms – including flattery and 'being nice'.

One form of manipulation is when people use 'conditional love' in order to get their needs met.

As adults, if we feel the need to manipulate others in order to get what we want it is time to question the ethics of our actions.

If we find that we are easily manipulated by others, it is time to ask what motivates us to do this, what do we get out of it, and what stops us from challenging our manipulator – what are we afraid of?

The need to manipulate in order to be in control is generated through fear, for instance the fear of losing control, or the fear of being discovered for who we really are.

ARROGANCE

This is a form of protection of a vulnerable person, they come across as 'bigger than self'. Their behaviour can be irritating and belittling if we don't see through it. If we react instead of responding rationally to this behaviour we have allowed it to affect us and our response is not likely to serve us, or them, well.

If we don't believe that we have ever been arrogant, or know how to be arrogant then try these behaviours out and notice how people begin to avoid you;

- give yourself a name or role that implies 'higher than thou,' when you haven't 'earned' it – director, leader, executive, guru, lecturer.

- blow your trumpet and tell everyone how wonderful you are and how you achieved something that others actually achieved.

- be condescending towards others – "A few more years and you might be able to do the job as good as me".

- belittle others pleasures in relation to yours – "So you went to the theatre to see Shakespeare, great. We were taken to see the Royal Shakespeare Company perform in Stratford, you really see a good performance there".

- be patronising - fail to appreciate the knowledge and experience that the other person has, acting as though you know better than they do – and that they need you to tell them.

Arrogance has no place in quality relationships.

"Should men however
fail to take up this search for
increased awareness
and no longer pursue freely a vision...

...these terrible healers
of plague,
disaster and war
move in to do it for them".

Sir Laurens Van der Post
Forward; Camphill and the shadow of our time
A CANDLE ON THE HILL
Edited by Cornelius Pietzner (1990)
Floris Books: UK

CONFLICT

Conflict arises through difference, that is different viewpoints, values, beliefs and practices. Many people associate conflict with experiences that are negative, damaging and difficult, they consequently avoid conflict. Conflict of this nature usually arises when force and power are used to 'resolve difference'.

Yet conflict brings a valuable contribution to our relationships when approached constructively. It is the grit in the oyster, the substance that builds robustness. When we face our conflict authentically and with integrity we will experience interactions that are rich and enabling with productive results, increased trust and greater appreciation of difference. Avoidance of conflict or force never achieves this.

Avoidance of dealing with conflict maintains a negative and destructive force in relationships often felt as an undercurrent which erupts at the most unexpected times.

Destructive conflict arises not because of difference but through;

- intolerance of difference
- mis-understandings in difference
- fear of difference and imagined consequences.

How we deal with conflict determines whether we face war or peace.

MANAGING CONFLICT

There is a very useful model that I draw on to deal with inter-personal conflict. It has never failed to help people to move forward.

For ease of description I refer to the people involved as **A** & **B**

1. Set the ground rules e.g. timeframes, confidentialities, owning what we say, and no interruptions. Both **A** & **B** should be encouraged to make reference to assumptions, expectations and interpretations that they are making.

2. **A** talks for an agreed time describing what it is like for them in the situation. **B** listens and if they want to can make notes.

3. **B** then seeks clarification on anything **A** might have said that they hadn't fully understand. **B** says how listening to **A** has left them feeling.

4. **A** and **B** swap their talking and listening roles.

5. **A** and **B** could repeat the talking and listening if they felt the need to.

6. When both **A** & **B** have heard each other and clarified misunderstandings, each person states how they would like to progress, coming to an agreement. This often is not needed as the work has progressed and is already changing.

7. Finally a date is agreed when **A** and **B** can review their progress.

The supporter's role in this exercise is to;

- hold each person to the ground rules, especially time boundaries
- encourage openness about thoughts, feelings and responses
- draw out expectations, assumptions and interpretations
- challenge personal attacks and judgements

HEALTHY COMPETITION

Healthy competition can be a powerful motivator that enables a person to achieve goals beyond their assumed limits.

In relating to others, healthy competition invites people to stretch their boundaries and to achieve their greatest potential.

Healthy competition carries with it mutual respect for others involved.

Healthy competition feeds progress.

Healthy competition is about being DIFFERENT.

UNHEALTHY COMPETITION

Some people feel the need to 'win' or 'be better than' in their relationships with others – rather than simply being different. If you are a persistent 'winner' then the chances are that ultimately you will lose.

What have you got to lose?

Just imagine living with someone who ALWAYS needs to win or get the better of you, who always had the 'right' answer or needed to have the 'last word'. You would likely feel second best, undervalued, dis-respected, not loved and not seen.

Ask yourself, are you a persistent winner?

What impact do you have on others when you seek to win an argument or have the last word in a discussion? Did you really listen to the other person, or were you protecting your own vulnerability?

There are consequences to unhealthy competition

- It's not so much WHAT persistent winners do, it is HOW they do what they do.

- The persistent winner focuses on themselves and their needs – which leads others to feel that their different viewpoint is not valued and respected.

- The persistent winner acts out of fear (i.e. a fear of losing)

Unhealthy competition dissolves the cohesiveness of relationships.

JUDGING

Our ability to judge ourselves in relation to others, and to make judgements about situations, is important both personally and socially. It is that process that enables us to make critical distinctions and achieve a balanced viewpoint.

Many difficult situations can be tracked back to judgements being made that were not balanced or fair. Mis-judgements arise when they are based on imaginings, on a stereotyped view of the world, on rumour or gossip, rather than accurate information.

When we pass judgement on others it says more about us than the other person.

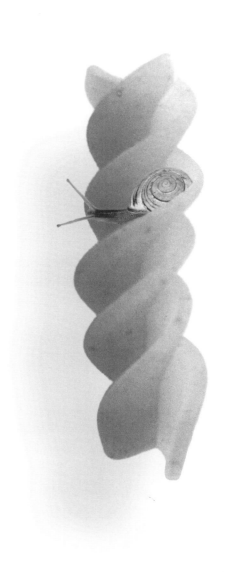

FUN

Fun only ever occurs in the moment even though we may have good memories of events in the past. Often when people say 'lets have some fun', it turns out to be quite the opposite. Equally, planned fun is never a certainty. I wonder why?

To have fun;

- we must be aware of what is fun for us personally and to tap into that part of ourselves. We are all different. What is fun for you might not be for others
- we must be in touch with our body. Fun is experienced in our body, not in our head
- we need to be spontaneous, yet trying to be spontaneous is a contradiction
- we need to be able to face our own humility, to accept (even delight in) our imperfections
- having fun is a release of energy, yet it often takes releasing of inner constraints in order to have fun. The idea of 'letting our hair down' is all about letting go of these personal constraints.
- Having fun at other people's expense is not acting with integrity.

We all have a sense of humour, sometimes this is buried deep and it takes others to help us find it.

People sometimes use their sense of humour to protect their vulnerability. They do this by cracking a joke instead of responding to a challenge or confrontation. This can impinge on relationships rather than adding value.

When people feel deeply sad and depressed one of the first things to vanish is their sense of humour and fun.

Having fun means being able to 'let go' of our inner constraints and tap into our free spiritedness.

CHOICE

We always have choice, in every act, every moment of every day. We have choice in the decisions that we make and how we respond to life's trials, tribulations, pleasures, disasters, and how we are in relation to others.

Sometimes we may feel that there is no choice when the route that we would like to take is blocked or circumstance don't provide us with favourable situations, yet we do have choice;

- in how we deal with loneliness
- in how we face a breakdown in relationships
- in how we deal with the death of a loved one
- in how we deal with our imperfections
- in how we address earths survival
- in how we deal with conflict
- in how, and if, we reveal our vulnerable self to others
- in how we deal with the consequences of making 'the wrong choice'
- in how we respond to circumstances that we didn't wish for or expect
- in how we live with our past
- in how you take in and use information from this book.

Notice that all of these statements are HOW statements. This highlights the point that many people feel disabled by their circumstances because they feel unable to change WHAT has happened. Focusing on HOW enables us to find our choice.

Making choices and acting on them means taking responsibility for the consequences of our actions.

Assuming no choice, is to become a victim of life.

Section 5
HABITS OF A LIFETIME

We are creatures of habit. Unfortunately
many of our behavioural habits are in
our bones and we fail to see how
they encroach on our relationships. Over
the years I have come to realise the
complex nature of deeply embedded
habitual behaviours on relationships.

WHAT'S UNFINISHED?

Until a few years ago it hadn't occurred to me that unfinished issues from the past could be so caustic in current relationships. At the time of my discovery I was questioning the dynamics that were getting in the way of a personal relationship. I recognised that I was unwittingly attempting to complete a difficult situation from the past that had nothing to do with the person in my current life. My past situation was incomplete, I had not had the courage to say what I really wanted to say at the time and the relationship ended unfinished. I began to see that my current relationship carried some of the hallmarks of the past, which unconsciously triggered an impulse to complete the past, unfinished 'stuff'. The dynamics were very confusing.

It then dawned on me the extent to which emotional drive in unfinished business gets in the way of relationships, not just historically, but also in our current everyday lives.

I noticed that people do not naturally develop the skills to complete interactions on a daily basis. When faced with difficult situations many people unconsciously or subconsciously avoid completing.

What is so significant is the level of emotional charge that exists in unfinished business that we are unaware of. When it is high we unconsciously attempt to complete in comparable situations. It invariably fails, so a pattern builds that leads to reactive behaviours that become fixed, as opposed to responsive, behaviours that are able to grow and adapt.

We can notice that unfinished business exists when our emotional change is out of balance with the situation.

I miss you
What you did was wrong
don't
you to
I did not understand
Thank you
I am sorry

FINISHING

In the first instance we can begin to acknowledge what is unfinished from the past with people that mattered. This should not be too difficult as most people remember unfinished situations due to the emotional charge that goes with them. These may come from today, yesterday, recent history, or from our early childhood.

There are things that we can do now that we were unable to do or say in the past even though that time is gone. The list is endless, here are a few finishing actions;

- say goodbye
- say thank you
- clarify misunderstandings and differences
- apologise
- forgive, or ask to be forgiven
- express disappointments
- give the other person feedback
- tell the other our truth.

In particular we need to ensure that we support ourselves well to do or say today what we were unable to complete in the past.

Sometimes people feel unable to complete because the other person is no longer alive or available. There are still things that we can do;

- write what we wanted to say in a letter, a poem, or a story with a symbolic completion like floating it out to sea, or burning it in a safe place
- draw a picture that symbolises what we want to say
- if they have died we could visit their grave and speak to the grave as though they can hear
- choose an object that most represents that person, or their photograph and talk to it.

Finishing unfinished business means letting go of the past.

LABELLING PEOPLE

We use a process of labelling people to help us make sense of the world and our social contact. It enables us to respond to collective values, to engage with groups and communities and to make inter-personal contact. Labels tend to contain generalisations about people and their roles, rather than name specific attributes.

Labelling can also cause mis-understanding, stress, conflict and pain in interpersonal relations when used thoughtlessly and when used rigidly. When labels become fixed people become stereotyped.

Labels get in the way of seeing people for who they really are;

- guru, King, Prince, Chief Executive
- English, Australian, French, American
- Moslem, Catholic, Protestant, Jew, agnostic
- bright, intelligent, pedantic, bossy
- boss, wife, daughter, doctor, gardener.

We all have many roles and many attributes that carry labels. Lifting labels enables us see the real person underneath.

Identifying with labels that are attributed to us stops us from growing and developing.

When we fix labels to people we diminish them.
When we fix labels to ourselves we diminish ourselves.

'On the one hand, when we discriminate we are making a carefully thought out choice of fine distinction between alternative actions or things.

On the other hand, when we discriminate we are acting on prejudice in a conditioned response to some person or event.'

Profiting from Diversity (1998)
Trevor Bentley & Susan Clayton

THE ART OF CARE-FULL DISCRIMINATION

Acting as though labels are 'true' leads to a fixed way of seeing both groups and individuals, we lose our ability to discriminate well.

When we discriminate badly we will act on a conditioned prejudice; a fixed belief, for instance 'men lack emotions', 'women lack intelligence'. This is care-less discrimination, which lacks truth.

When we discriminate well we are making a carefully thought out distinction between one person and another. People will feel that we care about them.

Careful discrimination enables informed choice.

you're blue!

WHAT'S PROJECTION?

Projection is like projecting images onto a screen and then acting according to what we see. We are the projector, the images come from within us and the screen is the other person. A very simple example of this is;

Imagine that you are with a friend and you want a cup of tea.

Instead of saying "I would like a cup of tea", you ask your friend 'would you like a cup of tea?" as though it is your friend that wants one.

Unhealthy projection is an impulse to escape a personal feeling, quality or behaviour that feels uncomfortable. In an attempt to escape the impulse, we project it onto another person, which we then see in them (on the screen).

Disowned feeling or behaviour	Projection onto other
frustration	we see others as frustrating
rejection of others	we feel rejected by others
unable to take responsibility for our actions	we blame others when things go wrong
unable to accept a caring part of ourselves	we commend others for being caring

We can notice our own projections when we use words like;

You   'You are not to be trusted
         rather than 'I feel unable to trust my judgement of you'

They   'They are unwieldy'
         rather than "I feel out of control of the situation'.

It   It is depressing'
         rather than 'I am feeling depressed'

He/She 'He is insensitive'
         rather than 'I don't feel appreciated by him'

When we are aware of our projections we can deal with them within ourselves and also check the assumptions that we make about others.

Projection weakens authenticity and can lead to many misunderstandings in relationships.

I am white!

"WE are blue"

ASSUMING SIMILARITY

When we seek sameness with others we often do so out of a sense of fear, and that gets in the way. We attempt to connect with others through patterns of behaviour and language that **assumes** sameness. We might even project something onto others that makes them appear the same as us.

We will know when this is happening because our language will include words like, 'we', 'they', 'us', 'everyone', 'one', 'the family...', 'the team ...', instead of what we really mean, 'I'. For example

- "they want to change the date"
- "we had a wonderful time on holiday"
- "everyone here is happy to stay late"
- "we are all really fed up with not knowing"

When this happens to us our personal struggle is in being seen as different, in accepting, trusting and valuing our own difference. Our fear is rejection or abandonment. The underlying mis-belief goes something like this; 'if we are all the same I will be accepted' or 'if they are accepted and I am the same as them, I will not be abandoned'.

There are times when fitting in is desirable and necessary. When it isn't necessary the beautiful tapestry of difference is diminished.

BELONGING

We all need to feel that we belong, some of us much more than others.

Belonging is simply to do with;

- being accepted for who we truly are
- being valued
- being appreciated
- being loved and cared about
- being understood
- practising common values
- carrying common beliefs

When I notice that groups of people that I am working with behave the same as each other and resist their difference I invite them to imagine looking around the group and to see themselves in everyone. I say 'imagine that everyone is YOU'. This exercise never fails to leave people feeling a huge sense of discomfort and to begin to value difference more.

'People are willing to give up their individuality, to suppress their potential, to hide their uniqueness and to mask their self identity for the sake of belonging, if that is the only way that they can find it. The need to belong is deep'.

Profiting from Diversity
Trevor Bentley and Susan Clayton

SWALLOWING RULES

Food that is selected, well chewed and digested nourishes us, whereas food that is swallowed whole indiscriminately is difficult to digest and lies heavy in the stomach. Much of our learning in life is similar. When we are selective about what we learn and allow time to digest our learning, we can assimilate it well.

There are, however, times in our lives when we are overwhelmed by messages enforced on us either through an authority figure (parent, teacher, boss). We are force fed with messages like; 'you are no good at music so don't try', 'girls must be seen and not heard', 'managers must act with authority'. The result is that we were unable to digest, chew over and discard what was not useful at the time. And then, later in life do not recognise that we have swallowed such a message that rules our lives. These messages become undigested but we tend to act in a way that reinforces them rather than challenges them. We become stuck and then project them out onto the world, onto other people.

So what fixed internal rules are likely to affect relationships? There are many, here are a few examples;

- I must not show my emotions
- Don't trust anyone
- I must not become angry
- People always get criticised for having opinions of their own, therefore I must be agreeable with others
- If I tell people what I really think they will reject me

As you can imagine suppressing impulses and holding back on emotions takes considerable restraint, which then impacts our relationships.

When we act on undigested messages we are more
concerned with what we or others should do, or have
to do rather than what we want to do.

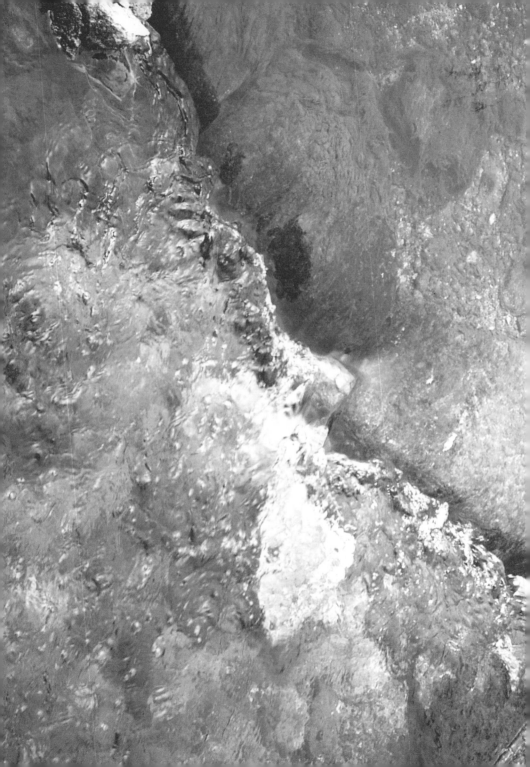

HOLDING BACK

There are a number of gestures that describe a behaviour of holding back;

- Biting your tongue
- Clenching your fist
- Shrugging your shoulders
- Swallowing hard

Some people believe that the opposite of holding back is a constant chatter. However, this may also be a way of not saying what we really want to say.

There are many reasons why we stop ourselves from speaking out, usually associated with fear. Yet holding back invites others to make assumptions about us. They may well interpret us wrongly.

On the other hand if we notice that others are saying very little we can bring in our own response to their silence;

- 'I am curious about your silence, I imagine that you all have something to say about this'.
- 'You aren't saying anything and I imagine that you have strong views on the subject'.

If we find ourselves regularly regretting not saying something that we really wanted to say, it is worth asking ourselves what stopped us from saying it at the time.

We also have choice, even after the event;

- We can go back to the person and say what we really want to say, for example "I've had some thoughts since our discussion which I would like to share with you"

  "there is something that I really want to say to you that I didn't say the other day...."

- We can practice a process of reflection and work towards bringing our thoughts into the present moment. The more we reflect and share our thoughts with others, the more we will trust our inner self and our spontaneously.

Withholding something that we really want to say
usually shows up somewhere in the body.

OUR UNIQUE PATTERNS

Have you ever noticed that your pattern of behaviour changes in different settings? For example I can be quite shy in groups of people that I don't know well but with people that I know well I can be much more outgoing and lively – even outrageous sometimes. I also notice how some people can spark off a very creative side of me, which becomes dulled by people who try to control me. We all experience this but few people are fully aware of the impact on their relationships.

Until we become more aware of the range of characteristics within us and how they are played out, our responses to different situations will be reactive rather than through choice.

We can increase our awareness by reflecting on a number of different situations and in each situation notice what's missing (which part of us do people *not* see). For instance we can compare at home, at work, with our extended family, with friends, and on holiday. Then ask ourselves how this affects the way that people relate to us.

In our relationships with others we can be curious about what we
don't see as well as what we do see in them. For most people
there is a lot more behind the façade; stories that
fascinate, abilities and interests that inspire, qualities
that impress, characteristics that delight.

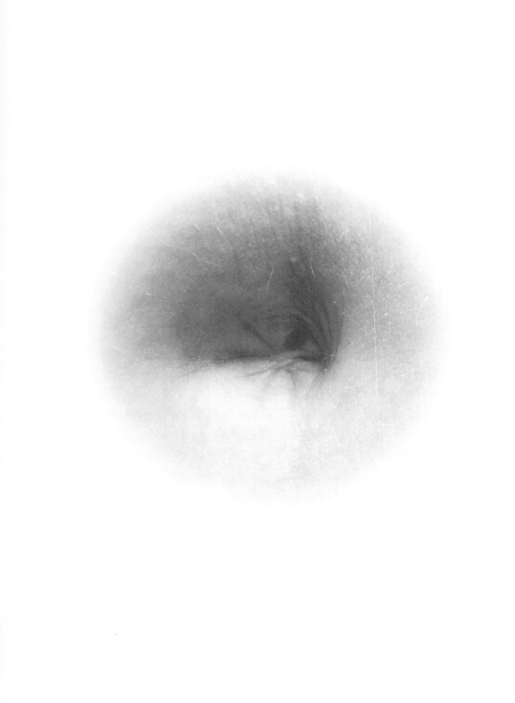

THE ENTANGLEMENT

Life is such that we can find ourselves in situations that seem entangled. We feel tied up in knots and cannot work out how to untie ourselves. The situation is both constraining and unsatisfactory.

Have you ever had to untangle a fishing line, a piece of string or a ball of wool. Trying to undo the knot takes time, patience and some skilful handling. Entangled relationships take an equal amount of patience.

The easiest thread to unravel in our entanglements is to look at ourselves because we can choose to change. We can ask 'what am I doing here that causes me so much difficulty?' or 'what am I NOT doing?'. The most difficult route is to attempt to change others. The more we try to change other people to become who we want them to be, the more entangled and dis-satisfying the relationship becomes.

There is a saying that has served me well and often stopped me in my tracks when I find myself repeatedly doing the same thing to no avail.

IF WE ALWAYS DO WHAT WE ALWAYS DID, WE WILL ALWAYS GET WHAT WE ALWAYS GOT.

When I hear this, and it takes a while sometimes for my frustrations to increase enough to want to hear it, then I can begin to be creative in untangling the situation.

Disentangling skills and actions look like this-

- I question my motives
- I question my authenticity and integrity
- I listen to others more and I seek to be heard
- I question what I am afraid of, what my worse fears are
- I look at my own behaviour and emotional energy driving me
- I ask what I might be contributing to the situation
- I become more imaginative in the way I engage with the people involved

Paradoxically, when we begin to really listen to other people, and feel heard ourselves, entanglements begin to unravel themselves.

THE DRAMA TRIANGLE

There is a complex and confusing drama that many people become caught in, I know it well, I have been caught in it too. It is called a drama triangle because three parts are 'played out'. These parts draw on fixed habitual patterns that sustain the triangle rather than break it.

They can be named in many ways, I name them here as;

The Villain
The Victim
The Hero

The Villain is the persecutor who finds their power and status through putting other people down.

The Victim is the person who is put down, or always the one who 'appears to suffer from the actions of others'. They appeal to other people's sympathy for their own comfort.

The Hero establishes acclaim for their 'goodness', always there to rescue the victim and offer 'support'. The sort of support that they offer colludes with the situation rather than breaking the drama.

It is not unusual for people to flip from one role to another, for instance from being a victim to becoming a hero, or from persecutor to victim. As you can imagine, this drama is both restrictive and destructive to relationships.

It only takes one person to break the drama triangle. To do so means becoming aware of our role and motives by asking ourselves questions like;

- What am I getting out of playing this role and how do I stay stuck?
- How can I get my needs met in other ways that help me grow?
- What would be the most loving and caring thing to do towards the other people in this drama?

169

Section 6
SETTING THE SCENE

'We teach them [people] how to live
authentically – the truthful spontaneity of
immediate improvisation – from their hearts
and gusts, from their longings and laughter. And
in turn we experience the revealed beauty'

Joseph C Zinker (1994)
In Search of Good Form

Consider the possibility that life is one great
big drama and that everything in this book has
been our guide into BEING on our stage.

However the conundrum is;
are we at rehearsal or is this the real thing?

If today is a rehearsal for tomorrow,
then what is tomorrow?

'All the world's a stage
and all the men and women merely players
They have their exits and their entrances
And one man in his time plays many parts.'

ASYOU LIKE IT
William Shakespeare

YOUR STAGE

The environment in which we live and work influences us and our relationships. Our surroundings, our home, our workplace, the community where we live, the places that we like to visit, the world at large – this is our stage.

In order to know our stage we can ask ourselves a series of questions;

- How does living and working in these places impact the relationships that I have?

- What do these places look like?

- How do they affect me?

- How do they reflect me as a person?

- What do I love about them?

- What do I dislike about them?

- What can I change?

- What's missing?

- How do I influence my stage?

Notice the level of importance that you give to artefacts around you in your home. These (or the lack of them) are all symbolic of who you are.

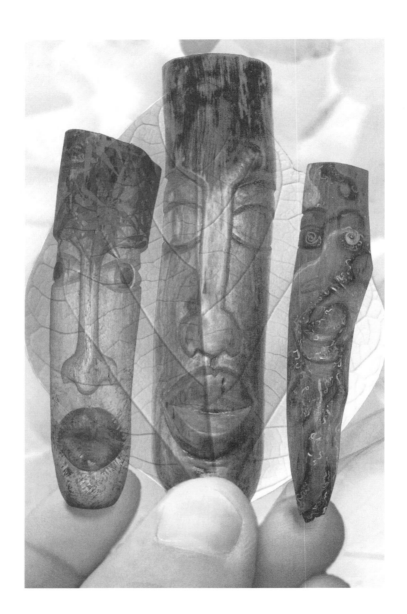

THE CHARACTERS

In this book I have made the point that life is co-created with people that we meet along the way. It is happening now as we read this book, we and I are co-creating a moment in our lives. That is a powerful position to be in because we are equal in this life drama. In truth neither you nor I have a part that is superior or inferior to the other. And the delight of this moment is that we are different. So I can appeal to you and you can appeal to me – without someone to read my book I am not an author, without a book to read you are not a reader or learner. We co-create this moment together.

Each person that we meet on our life journey we co-create the drama of that encounter. And the starting point is one of equality. What we impose on the moment and what is imposed on us, IS the drama, is life.

Who are the characters that interact with you on your stage?

Your family, work colleagues, the public, associates, distant friends, people that you see but don't know.

- Who are the people that you most interact with daily?
- Who are the people that you are in contact with in your work?
- Where are the most fulfilling and easiest contacts?
- With whom do you have the most difficult or challenging contact?
- Where are the people who are missing from your life drama and how does their absence affect you?
- How do your interactions with different people influence who you are?

Given that every encounter co-creates the real drama of life in each moment, notice what happens with the next person that you engage with, especially notice the finer points of your contact.

YOUR COSTUMES

What is your costume? What do people see when they meet you? Do you wear a wide range of costumes or simply a few? How much do you shine through your costume? How much are you affected by what other people wear?

There are a lot of sayings that begin to help us understand our layers of costumes that people see;

- he wears his heart on his shoulder
- she has a tough outer shell, it's hard to know what she is thinking or feeling
- he is a knight in shining armour
- she has a colourful personality

We wear our clothes and hairstyles in a way that are representative of us, whether we pay attention to this or not. The beggar on the street creates his character in what he wears as much as a king in his castle.

Notice your own costumes;

- How do they reflect who you are?
- Do you choose what you wear?
- Does your personality shine through or does your external persona disguise the inner you?
- Do you wear different costumes for different settings? Are you expected to wear a uniform at work, if so how do you personalise this?
- To what extent have your costumes changed over the years?
- How do your clothes affect the way that people relate to you?

Do you wear your costumes because you love them, or because you think others will love them?

YOUR MASK

Let's assume that our face is your mask, a mask of many changing expressions. Masks can act in two ways, to hide our inner selves and also to bring our inner selves into full character. Our mask has a powerful impact on the way that people relate to us.

Many years ago I learned about my own mask when someone said to me "you always wear a smile on your face and I don't believe it."

This was hard for me to hear yet it made me realise how my cheeks ached with smiling so much. I was wearing a mask which I believed would secure my need to be liked, but of course it didn't. People found it difficult to interact with me because they didn't know what I was really feeling or thinking behind my fixed smile.

Although I felt at risk to emerge from my hideaway, I have since discovered how rewarding it is to be fully me, and also that I have choice.

Our different facial expressions reveal us and also hide us. For example I notice in my work I am more serious than when I am with intimate friends, I have a serious look that goes with this – which people respond to in a serious way. My serious work mask hides a more intimate part of me that is mischievous, witty and fun.

Removing false masks and bringing ourselves more fully into our life drama increases our authenticity. We can do this through becoming aware of how we are in different situations, how we behave, what we hide away, what people see of us and don't see of us.

Other people might observe differences in us if they see us in different contexts but we are the only person who knows those differences. We are the only person who is in charge of our masks.

Our mask has the capacity to express our inner selves without words.

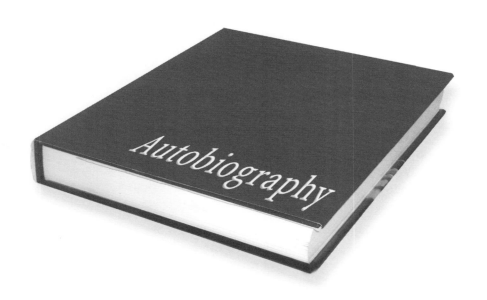

YOUR STORYLINE

Our past, our history and our future aspirations are all held in the present moment, held in our storyline as our autobiography unfolds.

Notice how your life drama has unfolded already and how much other people have played a part in your storyline. Consider also how your plans for the future affect what you do today.

However your storyline isn't only about what exists. Stories are also about the space between what is told and what is untold. So your story is also about what is missing, what is unspoken.

Notice as you read this book how it too becomes part of your life story. Once something exists in our lives we cannot take it away.

Small is beautiful

Two plus one

Family entanglements

The land of grin

Four wheels and a dragon

om head to heart

From head to heart

Discovering how to BE

Ouch!

Getting there

Alone at sea

Travelling light

beautiful

Perplexed

Getting there

YOUR TITLE

When you think of your life so far what title would you give it?

Is your storyline full of mystery, is it thrilling, romantic, devastating. Is it a musical or pantomime? Does it have imagination?

Where do power, control and manipulation come into your biography? Where is humour, joy, fear, passion, hunger and grief?

Who are the villains and heroes?

What is real and what is imagined, what is fact and what is fiction?

How well do others feature in our relationships with family, friends and intimate personal relationships?

Your title is as important as your name.

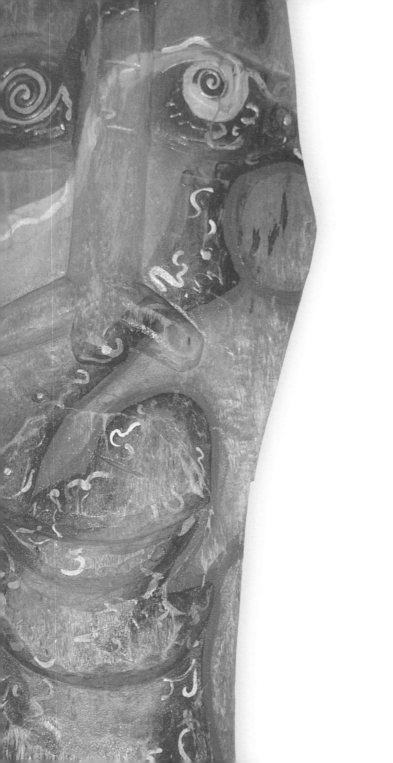

THE UNFOLDING MYSTERY

The unfolding mystery, the unpredictability of the dynamic world that we live in, and our relationships, are what gives us a storyline. This drama has a mystery to it that no-one knows. As far as we know in our linear existence we do not have the storyline in advance only that which has passed. We create it as we live. And we are all in the same predicament.

We may not be able to pre-determine our destiny for that is what it becomes. But we can influence and impact our unfolding drama through increased awareness and through learning how to become more skilled in relating with others.

The space between is where the mystery unfolds

About the Author

Susan Clayton is a Chartered Psychologist practicing in business and organisation development. Most of her work today is in developing top people and executive teams. She is a founding partner of *the space between* in the UK and *the space between Australia.*

Susan is a leading proponent of Gestalt in Organisations, a growing field of consulting and organisation development worldwide. Her learning and teaching in this area has provided a major source of inspiration and understanding about people and the way that we inter-relate.

You can contact Sue at *the space between*
Email: sue@thespacebetween.com

About the Designer

Vicki Clayton founded Waimanu Creative Design in 1999. Her unique designs are used for book covers, web pages, marketing material and assignments where a metaphor or visual message can enhance a subject.

Vicki gains inspiration for her work from nature and natural form. She has travelled widely and draws on her experience with different cultures for ideas and creativity.

You can contact Vicki at Waimanu Creative Design
Email: vicki@waimanu.com